OUR PLANET

SO-ALI-459

Oceans

CALLY OLDERSHAW

Troll Associates

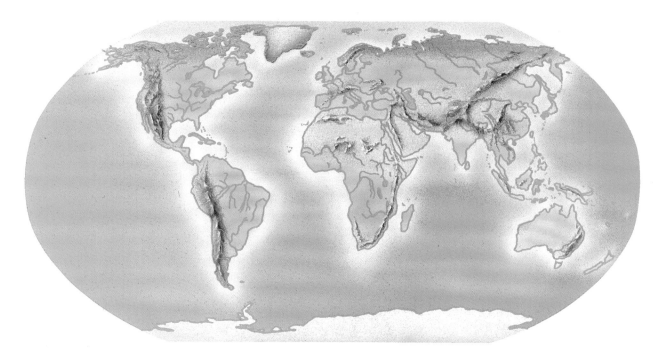

Library of Congress Cataloging-in-Publication Data

Oldershaw, Callie.
    Oceans / by Callie Oldershaw ; illustrated by Robert Burns ... [et al.].
       p.   cm. — (Our planet)
    Summary: Describes the physical characteristics, plants and animals, resources, pollution, and conservation of the world's oceans.
    ISBN 0-8167-2753-8 (lib. bdg.)   ISBN 0-8167-2754-6 (pbk.)
    1. Ocean—Juvenile literature.   [1. Ocean.]   I. Burns, Robert, ill. II. Title. III. Series.
GC21.5.053 1993
551.46—dc20   91-45079

Published by Troll Associates

Edited by Neil Morris and Kate Woodhouse

Design by Sally Boothroyd

Picture research by Jan Croot

Printed in the U.S.A.

10 9 8 7 6 5 4 3 2

Illustrators
Robert Burns: 4-5, 6-7, 9, 19, 22-23
Martin Camm: 12, 28
Mike Roffe: 11, 18-19, 20-21
Phil Weare: 12-13, 16-17

Picture credits
Gamma: 26
GSF Picture Library: 7, 8, 8-9, 10-11, 14, 24, 26-27, 28
Craig Hamm 19
NHPA: 17
NHPA: Stephen Krasemann: 14-15
NHPA: John Shaw: 13
John Noble: 6
Spectrum: 28-29
Tony Waltham: 1, 20, 22-23
ZEFA: 4-5, 21, 22, 24-25

Cover photo: Waves crashing on rocks

Title page:
Waves of the Atlantic Ocean breaking against the coast of Ireland.

CONTENTS

Beginnings

From the moon our planet looks blue. This is because nearly three-quarters of Earth is covered with water. There are three major oceans and many seas which connect to form one world ocean.

It has not always been like this. When Earth was formed about 4.6 billion years ago, there was no water. It did not rain for millions of years. Scientists believe the first oceans and seas were made when steam from volcanoes turned to rain and filled the craters made by meteorites that had crashed into Earth. Water was one of the things that made Earth different from the other planets. It meant plants and animals could live and survive on Earth.

Earth has an outer shell made of plates that fit together like a jigsaw puzzle. The shape and size of the oceans and the ocean floor change as the plates move. Two hundred million years ago there was only one ocean, and the land formed one large continent called Pangaea. Pangaea's plate split into two, Laurasia and Gondwanaland. These split further, and over millions of years some plates joined again until the continents became as they are now. Compare the coastlines of Europe and Africa with the coastlines of North and South America and you can see how they fit together. Now Europe and Africa are thousands of miles apart from North and South America, and they are moving about 1½ inches (4 centimeters) farther apart each year.

▶ Continents on different plates move apart when new oceanic crust is formed. This new crust is formed at the oceanic ridge. Volcanoes and earthquakes are produced where the oceanic crust and continental crust meet near the edge of the ocean.

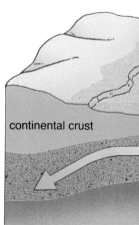

continental crust

◀ Iceland is a volcanic island on the mid-Atlantic spreading ridge. Molten magma rises from Earth's interior and erupts as lava from volcanoes. At Heimaey, hot black lava flows down the side of the volcano to the sea. When the lava reaches the sea it cools and hardens, which changes the shape of the coastline.

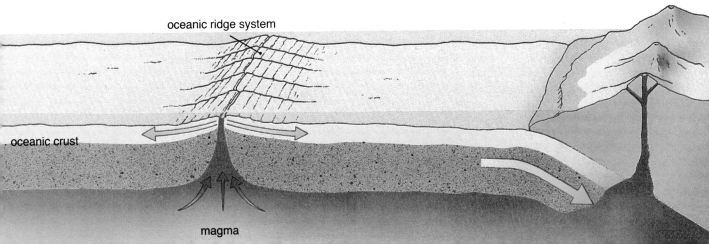

oceanic ridge system

oceanic crust

magma

The sea and the weather

Nearness to an ocean can affect weather and climate. Although Chicago, Illinois is farther south than Plymouth, England, the climate in England is milder because of the warmth of the Gulf Stream. Chicago, which is far from any ocean, tends to have greater extremes of temperature.

The sea can be the source of violent weather.

▲ The oceans of Antarctica are so cold that some parts are permanently frozen.

▶ When the sun shines on the sea, surface water evaporates and rises to form clouds. When the clouds reach colder air over land they release rain. The rain flows into rivers which carry the water back to the sea.

Typhoons and hurricanes are whirling storms that begin at sea and may be blown inland, where they can cause great damage. *Tsunamis* are waves started by an underwater earthquake or a volcanic eruption. The waves travel very fast. In the ocean they may be small, but when they reach the shore, the water can build up to a great height. In 1876, for example, a tsunami in the Bay of Bengal killed 200,000 people when it reached shore.

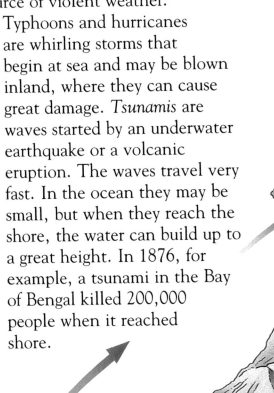

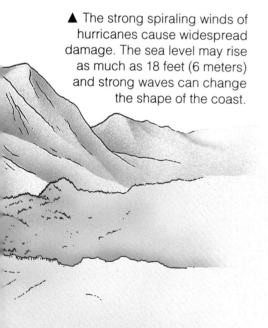

▲ The strong spiraling winds of hurricanes cause widespread damage. The sea level may rise as much as 18 feet (6 meters) and strong waves can change the shape of the coast.

The total amount of water in the oceans and seas has not changed for about three billion years. Water is not lost, but goes around the *water cycle* and is used again and again. However, the depth and shape of the sea and land does change. For example, the level of the sea is lower when water is frozen and trapped on the land as snow and ice.

Many scientists believe that Earth is getting warmer. If the average temperature of Earth were to rise by only 4.9°F (2.7°C), ice in the polar regions would gradually melt. The level of the sea would rise about 3 feet (one meter) and much of London and New York City would be underwater.

Water

The oceans rarely stay still. Usually there is a wind blowing across the water making small ripples or larger waves. When the waves reach land, they break on the shore. The level at which waves break on the beach varies according to the tide. The twice-daily tides are caused by the *gravitational pull* of the moon and the sun. At some places on the Atlantic coast the tide may rise and fall 50 feet (15 meters), but in the Mediterranean Sea there is no real tide. The average tide is about 6 feet (two meters).

▲ The wet pebbles, darkened by the sea, mark the line that the sea reached at high tide.

When you swim in the sea, you will notice that the temperature of the water varies from place to place, and that the water is salty. The surface water is warmed by the sun, but deeper water stays cold. Light and heat from the sun cannot reach the depths of the ocean, which are always cold and in total darkness. The amount of salt in the sea is called its *salinity*. There are usually about 35 parts of salt to every 1,000 parts of water. The sea is twice as salty as our tears. The saltiness of the sea makes it easier to float when you are swimming. The Dead Sea is very salty: You can lie back and read a book without sinking!

Currents are simply water that is moving from one place to another. Currents vary according to the water's temperature and salinity. Deep ocean currents may travel in the opposite direction to shallow currents above them.

▲ As the tide rises, the sea will cover many of the rocks on this coast of Brittany in France.

▶ Tides are caused by the pull of gravity on the oceans from the sun and the moon. When the sun, moon, and Earth are in a line, the pull is greater and the tides are larger than usual. This happens twice a month, at full moon (as in the diagram) and when there is a new moon. These tides are called spring tides. Neap tides are smaller than usual and also occur twice a month between the spring tides.

9

The shape of the coasts

On the coast, where the sea meets the land, there are steep cliffs, rocky shores, or sandy beaches. The waves of the sea attack the coasts, carving them into many shapes and gradually wearing them away. In some places, such as Norway and Greenland, there are long *fjords*, or inlets, where the sea has flooded glacier valleys. Nordvest Fjord in Greenland extends 195 miles (313 kilometers) inland.

Hard rocks, such as basalt or granite, form high cliffs. When the cliffs are battered by the sea, large rocks come crashing down. The action of the waves breaks the rocks first into rounded pebbles and eventually into sand. Softer rocks, such as white chalk cliffs, are worn away more quickly.

The color of sand may give a clue to the rocks from which it was made. Black sand may be from old volcanic lava. White sand is often made of millions of crushed skeletons and the shells of dead animals from the sea. White sand is also formed from *quartz*, a mineral found in many rocks.

The sea is always battering the coastline. Beaches change shape too. The sea can move sand away from the beach or along the coast from one beach to another. Breakwaters are sometimes built to try to prevent beaches from losing their sand. Sand may also protect the coast by building up sandy barrier islands offshore, which lessen the force of the waves against the coast.

▶ The steep cliffs, headlands, and bays of this coast in California have been formed by the action of the sea. The waves wear away the softer rocks before the harder rocks.

basalt

◀ The sands on this beach in Hawaii are made from black lava. The lava erupted from volcanoes and waves have broken it down into sand.

Life on the seashore

The shore reaches from the lowest point uncovered by the tide to the highest sea-washed point on land. The shore may be mud, sand, or rock, and each has its own particular group of plants and animals. Sandy shores are alive with worms and shrimps wriggling in and out of the sand. Don't bother to look for animals on a pebble beach. They cannot survive there because the pebbles move with the tide. If you look carefully in rock pools, there might be seaweeds, crabs, seashells, starfish, fish, or even sea slugs!

Birds nest on rocks and steep cliffs, where they are safe from land enemies. Their only enemies are other, larger birds. They also have a rich source of food nearby, with fish from the sea and worms and insects from the shore.

▶ Starfish, prawns, crabs, limpets, periwinkles, whelks, sea anemones, seaweed, and barnacles survive in or beside tidal rock pools. They are never far from the sea.

▲ Puffins live in large groups on cliffs. They dive and swim underwater to catch fish.

◄ A blood starfish sheltering in a tidal rock pool. It must wait for the tide to rise before it can move through the water to another pool.

Animals and plants on the seashore must adapt to living in both water and air. Can you think of ways in which they have done this? Razor shells and sandmason worms bury themselves in the sand when the sea goes out. On rocky shores, barnacles, mussels, and snails hide in their shells and wait for the returning tide.

Seaweeds do not have roots like land plants. They have *holdfasts* which cling to the rocks, but do not take food from the rocks. Holdfasts provide shelter to many smaller plants and animals on the seashore. The seaweeds that live near the shore are tough and leathery, so they can survive for a short time out of water.

13

Life in the sea

There are millions of animals and plants living in the sea. They come in all sizes, from tiny plankton to the giant blue whale, the largest creature on Earth. There are friendly dolphins, dangerous sharks, and poisonous fish. Many fish are beautiful and brightly colored, while others are strange-looking or even terrifying. Fish, plants, and other animals live in the areas of the seas that suit them best.

▲ These crabeater seals can survive the cold waters of the Antarctic.

Marine mammals such as whales, porpoises, and dolphins spend their lives at sea, but cannot stay underwater all the time. They must swim to the surface to breathe air. A sperm whale, for example, can stay beneath the surface for about an hour without taking a breath, but then must surface to fill its lungs with air. Whales travel over very large areas. They spend the summer in warm waters, where their babies are born, then move to colder waters in search of food. Like other mammals, whales are warm-blooded, so they have a thick layer of blubber which keeps them warm in colder waters. Seals, which are also sea mammals, eat fish from the sea, but give birth and care for their young on land.

Green turtles are cold-blooded and cannot cope with different temperatures, so they follow warm currents of water, whose temperature hardly varies. Emperor penguins thrive in the very cold climate and frozen seas of the Antarctic. Corals, which look like plants but are limestone formations made by animals called polyps, can survive only in warm, shallow waters.

coral

▶ Walruses in the cold waters off Alaska.

14

Fish spend all their lives underwater. They keep to the depth and temperature of water that suits them best. Fish that live near the surface, where it is light, eat plankton and other fish. Plankton are tiny plants and animals that get their energy from sunlight. They must rise to the surface for the sunlight. Deeper down in the sea it is completely dark. When plankton die they sink, providing food for the fish that live in deeper water. Fish that eat plankton are in turn eaten by other fish. Most fish are meat-eaters. They hunt their prey by sight or smell, and some can feel the movement of other fish in the water.

The fish we eat are caught in the shallower waters of the continental shelf. Some, such as tuna and herring, live near the surface. Herring travel in schools several miles long and are caught in baglike nets. Haddock and cod keep to the ocean floor, where they are dragged up in trawl nets.

Beyond the continental shelf, the waters are much deeper. We know very little about the weird and wonderful creatures that live where it is always dark and cold. There are some fish that have no eyes and others that have eyes almost as big as their heads. Because there are no plants, the animals of the deep can only exist by eating each other. Some attract prey by using flashing lights, others have enormous jaws and can swallow prey bigger than themselves in a single gulp.

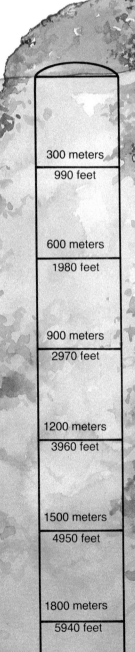

300 meters

990 feet

600 meters

1980 feet

900 meters

2970 feet

1200 meters

3960 feet

1500 meters

4950 feet

1800 meters

5940 feet

► These hatchetfish have enormous eyes to help them see in the dark depths of the sea.

▼ This diagram shows animals and plants living at different depths. Butterfly fish and sharks swim near the surface, while sperm whales and squid go much deeper.

Navigation and exploration

For hundreds of years people believed that Earth was flat, surrounded by water that ran over the edge. They thought that if they went too far, they would fall off. The sea was a dangerous place of terrifying tales, monsters, and superstitions. Ships sailing these dangerous waters needed plenty of good luck. The building, naming, and launching of a ship was considered to be very important. Sailors thought tattoos and earrings brought good luck, but hares and pigs brought bad luck.

▼ *Challenger* was a wooden warship, 250 feet (76 meters) long with both sails and a steam engine. Steam winches pulled up the long ropes attached to nets that collected animals and plants from the ocean depths.

▲ Sextants were early navigational instruments. Sailors could focus on the stars to determine direction.

People from early civilizations crossed seas and made maps. The Arabs and Greeks thought the world was round. They developed navigational equipment so that they could tell where they were, and they made maps of the Mediterranean Sea.

In 1492 Christopher Columbus tried to sail around the world. Instead, he reached a part of the world that was unknown to Europeans. The success of his voyage of discovery to America encouraged other expeditions to sail all the major oceans of the world. Other lands were discovered, and spices, silk, opium, tea, potatoes, and tobacco were brought back to Europe.

Many years later, people began to study the sea. *Oceanography* is the scientific study of oceans. The first well-planned expedition of scientific research was by the British ship *Challenger*, which sailed around the world between 1872 and 1876. The scientists on the ship gathered information, collected specimens, and took measurements. The results of their work were published in fifty books about the currents, underwater landscapes, sediments, and life of the deep sea.

▲ These "landers" gather information and video the ocean floor for scientists to study.

Modern sea transport

The seas were once great barriers, not only for people, but also for the migration of land and sea creatures. Kangaroos and other marsupials developed when Australia was completely cut off from the rest of the world. Now the oceans have become routes for travel, communication, and commerce. Bridges and tunnels have been built. Telecommunication cables run under the sea. Canals connect oceans separated by land.

▲ Container ships are an efficient means of transport. Some ships can carry 250 containers, which can be loaded on and off the ship very quickly.

In the last 150 years there have been great improvements in the design and building of ships. The supertanker is one of the most efficient forms of bulk transport in the world, taking into account the amount of cargo it can carry, the fuel it uses, and the distance it travels. However, it is not an easy ship to turn or control.

One of the world's most famous passenger ships was the *Titanic*. It was said to be unsinkable, but on its first voyage across the Atlantic in 1912, it struck an iceberg and sank, with the loss of 1,500 lives. There are still many passenger liners crossing the oceans, but more people today travel by air.

The modern sailor has the advantage of better charts and maps, navigation aids, communications, and worldwide weather forecasts. Space satellites orbit Earth and send back information about cloud cover and sea conditions. The invention of radar has meant fewer collisions and safer routes. Help to ships in distress is quicker, and fewer lives are lost at sea. Even so, the sea is powerful, dangerous, and unpredictable.

► Large, flat barges are used to transport vast amounts of oil across oceans.

▼ Hovercraft skim the surface of the water on a rubber air-filled cushion at speeds averaging 55 miles (90 kilometers) per hour. Hovercraft cannot operate on very rough seas, but they can travel on tidal mud flats, frozen ground, or ice-congested seas, where boats cannot go.

Food from the sea

Most of the fish we eat are taken from the sea in nets. In the past a country "owned" the seas along its coastline, out to a distance of three miles (five kilometers) — the distance that a cannonball could be shot. Nowadays international laws regulate where people may fish.

In the past twenty years many of the world's major fishing grounds have been overfished. Refrigerated factory ships and powerful machines for lifting nets have meant that even more fish are caught in deeper seas. Drift nets are many miles long, catching all the fish in their path. But often seals, porpoises, and other marine animals are also caught in the nets and drown.

▼ These fish are scooped out of the sea with a seine net and landed on the boat. To catch them, the boat circled the fish at high speed, while it let out its net. Then the bottom of the net was closed and the fish trapped.

drift

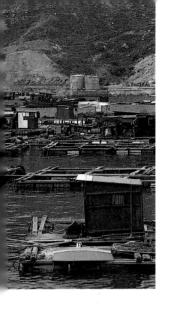

Scientists are researching ways of fishing in deeper waters for new and different types of fish. Russia and Japan harvest *krill* from the Antarctic. Krill are tiny, shrimplike creatures which are the main food of baleen whales and penguins. But if krill were to be overfished, baleen whales and penguins would be endangered. Another possibility is the expansion of fish farming. This is an ancient practice in which fish are bred in tanks or ponds, or in pens out at sea. Some of these fish are put back in the sea and others are sold straight from the farms. About one in ten of the world's fish is farmed, for use either as food or for restocking the seas.

▲ This fish farm is in Hong Kong. Fish live and grow in the nets that are hanging from under the rafts.

▼ Drift nets and long lines hang down from fishing boats. A long line may have 5,000 hooks, each with a bait to catch fish.

▼ Trawl nets and seine nets are towed by fishing boats. Different fish are caught using nets with different-sized holes.

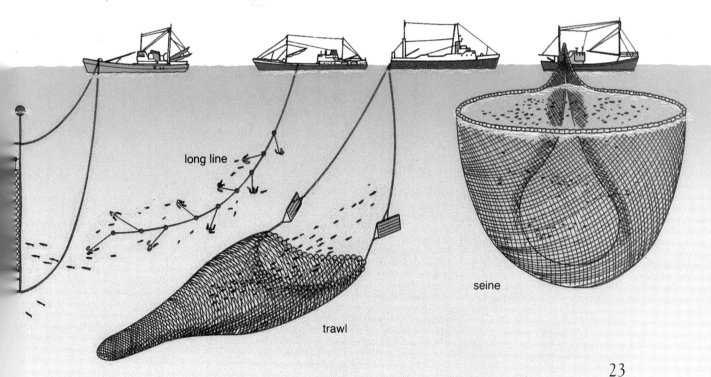

long line

trawl

seine

23

Mineral resources

The sea is not just salty water. There are many different chemicals in it, some solid and some liquid. Some can be seen on the sea floor or in the water. Some are out of sight under the sea floor and others are dissolved in the water. Many are in such small quantities that we cannot collect them. Minerals have either been deposited in rocks over millions of years, or they have been washed into the sea from the land. Sodium and chlorine are two of the minerals dissolved in the sea. Together they make salt. This salt can be taken out of seawater to make fresh water, which can then be used for drinking or irrigation, but this is an expensive process.

Shells, sand, gravel, and lumps of manganese and phosphorite can be scooped up from the sea bed by dredgers. Much of the dredged material is then thrown back, so that both the sea and the sea bed are disturbed.

Oil and gas make up about nine-tenths of all the minerals taken from the sea. They are found under the sea floor and have to be extracted by drilling. Oil is pumped ashore in underwater pipes or moved in tanker ships. Pipelines also carry gas. The extraction of oil and gas is both dangerous and expensive.

◀ Sea salt was the first mineral that early people collected from the sea. Salt is separated from the sea by evaporating seawater in large shallow pans called salt pans.

▲ Oil and gas were the first mineral resources taken from beneath the oceans. The first undersea oil was drilled off California in 1891. This modern oil rig is in the North Sea.

The energy in waves can be harnessed to generate electricity. Shoreline wave energy is particularly useful to small islands, and may be used more in the future.

Pollution

Unfortunately some people seem to think that the sea is an enormous garbage dump, where anything can be thrown away. Most *pollutants*, such as oil, pesticides, detergents, lead, and mercury, have been pumped into the sea through drains or sewage pipes. Others, including nuclear waste, have been dumped from ships.

▲ At wildlife centers, oil-soaked birds collected from polluted beaches after an oil spill are cleaned.

Oil spills account for only a small fraction of *pollution*. But oil is very destructive, because it smothers life in rock pools and kills hundreds of thousands of birds every year. Although the oil does eventually break down, detergents are often used to speed up the process. These may also be poisonous and cause further damage to the environment.

Many countries pump sewage into shallow water, which is then brought back with the incoming tide. Bacteria multiply rapidly in the warm, shallow waters where people swim. Chemicals and industrial waste are other pollutants. Factories near the sea or on rivers often discharge their waste products into water, which is then harmful for fish.

Out at sea, pollution takes other forms. Fishermen have found plastic cups in the stomachs of fish, and turtles have eaten plastic bags, which they thought were jellyfish. Plastic collars from canned drinks strangle birds and entangle the snouts of seals, causing them to starve or drown.

▼ Waste from a tin mine in Cornwall, England is discharged into the sea. This could cause a huge amount of damage to plant and wildlife.

The oceans and seas are a vital part of the environment and should not be polluted in any way. It would be easy to think the depths of the sea are not important, but no part of Earth can be separated from another part. What happens in the seas will also eventually affect the land.

Conservation and the future

The oceans give great pleasure to many people. There are beaches to play on, seas to swim in, rock pools to explore, beautiful views to admire. Oceans are so important to everyone that we must all work together to protect and preserve this natural environment. We need to learn how to protect the plants and animals of the seas from pollution and to save them from extinction.

One person alone cannot do this, but everyone can help. Governments and scientists must agree to work together to ensure that no more damage is done to the seas or to the animals and plants living in them. Clubs and school groups, as well as scientists, can plan conservation projects.

Many projects depend on the gathering of a great deal of information. For example, it might be useful to know how many gray whales passed a particular beach in California for two years running. This information would enable scientists to discover more about the condition of gray whales today.

▲ Windsurfing is just one of many enjoyable sea sports.

▶ Gray whales travel huge distances every year. We should all learn about whales, and other animals and plants of the oceans, so we can avoid harming them and their environment.

▲ These children playing with seaweed on a beach are looking for small animals and seashells. If they find any, they should not take them out of their damp protective covering, and the animals should be replaced where they were found.

The sea should be enjoyed by everyone. It is a vital part of Earth's environment and essential for our pleasure and food. We must look after it and make sure that it is not spoiled for people in the future.

Fact file

Earth's surface
The seas cover approximately 71 percent of Earth's surface. The largest ocean in the world, the Pacific, covers nearly 46 percent.

Freshwater
Ninety-seven percent of Earth's water is in the oceans. Only 3 percent is fresh water. The total water supply on Earth has remained the same for 3,000 million years.

Depth
The average depth of the sea is about 13,700 feet (4,175 meters), compared with an average land height of about 2,800 feet (853 meters). The deepest part of the ocean is the Mariana Trench in the Pacific Ocean, which is about 36,200 feet (11,036 meters) deep.

The dark oceans
Ninety-nine percent of the sea is in perpetual darkness. On average, sunlight only reaches the top 600 feet (180 meters) of the sea.

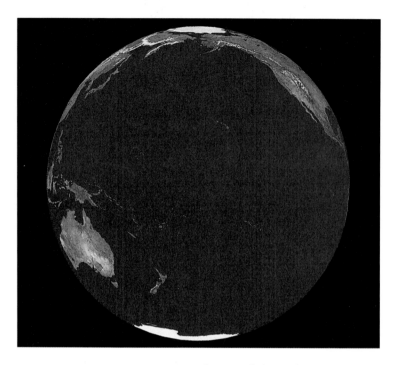

▲ A satellite picture of the Pacific Ocean.

▼ Giant kelp on the Falkland Islands in the South Atlantic.

Largest living animal
The blue whale is the largest living animal. It can be over 100 feet (30 meters) long and weigh 160 tons (metric tons).

Largest sea plant
The giant kelp is the largest sea plant, growing up to 196 feet (60 meters) long. There are forests of kelp that cover more than 1,000 square miles (2,600 square kilometers) near Shark Bay, off the coast of western Australia.

Salinity
The Atlantic Ocean is the warmest and the saltiest of the major oceans, and the Pacific is the coolest and least salty. Although seawater is always salty before it freezes, the ice is freshwater.

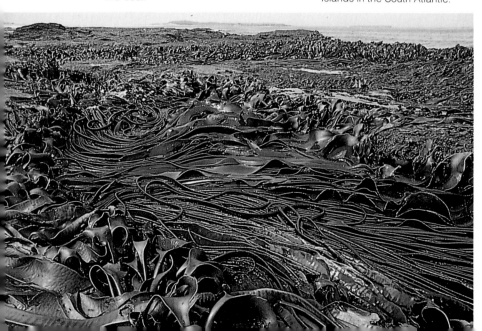

Underwater mountain chain
The longest single feature of Earth's surface was only discovered in this century. It is an underwater mountain chain called the oceanic ridge system. It is more than 37,000 miles (60,000 kilometers) wide and 47,000 miles (76,000 kilometers) long.

Temperature
The temperature of the deep waters of the oceans is about 38°F (3.3°C). The surface water of the polar seas can be as cold as 28°F (−2°C), and tropical seas can be as warm as 96°F (36°C).

Sea's fastest hunters
Tuna fish are the sea's fastest hunters. They can swim up to 70 miles (110 kilometers) per hour.

Tides
Spring is the highest tide and *neap* is the lowest tide. Spring comes from the Old English word meaning swell, and neap is from the Old English word meaning scarcity.

▲ A gray nurse shark off the coast of Australia.

Sargasso Sea
The Sargasso Sea is in the Atlantic Ocean. It has weak currents, and great quantities of seaweed grow there. It is also the breeding ground for the common eel. After about 10 years in rivers, female eels swim to the Sargasso Sea to lay their eggs and die. The young eels then swim all the way to Europe and North America.

Fossil relatives
Some of the oldest animals of Earth live in the sea. Fossils of the horseshoe crab have been found that are millions of years old and horseshoe crabs still exist today. Sharks have also changed very little over millions of years. The first sharks swam in ancient oceans more than 250 million years ago. Today they are the largest fish in the oceans.

▼ A horseshoe crab.

Index